Nonprofit Quick Guide™

How to Answer the Eight Questions Every Grant Review Committee Asks

Joanne Oppelt, MHA
Linda Lysakowski, ACFRE

Nonprofit Quick Guide: How to Answer the Eight Questions Every Grant Review Committee Asks

One of the **Nonprofit Quick Guide™** series

Published by Joanne Oppelt Consulting, LLC

Copyright © 2020 by Joanne Oppelt and Linda Lysakowski

All rights reserved. No part of this book shall be reproduced, stored in a retrieval system, or transmitted by any means, electronic, mechanical, photocopying, recording, or otherwise, without written permission from the publisher. No patent liability is assumed with respect to the use of the information contained herein. This publication contains the opinions and ideas of its author. It is intended to provide helpful and informative material on the subject matter covered. It is sold with the understanding that the author and publisher are not engaged in rendering professional services in the book. If the reader requires personal assistance or advice, a competent professional should be consulted. The author and publisher specifically disclaim any responsibility for any liability, loss, or risk, personal or otherwise, that is incurred as a consequence, directly or indirectly, of the use and application of any of the contents of this book. Although every precaution has been taken in the preparation of this book, the publisher and author assume no responsibility for errors or omissions. No liability is assumed for damages resulting from the use of information contained herein.

ISBN Print Book: 978-1-951978-03-7

13 12 11 10 9 8 7 6 5 4 3 2 1

Printed in the United States of America

About the Authors

JOANNE OPPELT, MHA

Joanne, principal of Joanne Oppelt Consulting, LLC, is a seasoned rainmaker with a distinguished track record of success. During her twenty-five-plus years working in the nonprofit arena, she built or rebuilt successful fundraising departments at every stop, helping her organizations grow capacity and more effectively fulfill their missions.

She has held positions from grant writer to executive director at the nonprofits Community Access Unlimited, Caring Contact: A Listening Community, Family to Family Network of New Jersey, Christian Healthcare Center, March of Dimes Central New Jersey, Prevent Child Abuse New Jersey, and Maternal and Family Health Services. Her extensive background in a variety of work roles and organizations enables her to understand the realities and challenges nonprofit practitioners face–both internally and externally. Her success at every stop positions her to help any nonprofit, whether through her books or consulting practice, turn around its struggling fundraising operations.

Joanne is the author of four books and coauthor of four others. She has taught at Kean University as an Adjunct Professor in its graduate program. She is also a highly sought-after speaker and presenter.

Joanne holds a master's degree in health administration from Wilkes University, where she graduated with distinction. Her bachelor's degree is in education, with a minor in psychology.

LINDA LYSAKOWSKI, ACFRE

Linda is one of approximately one hundred professionals worldwide to hold the Advanced Certified Fundraising Executive designation. Linda is the author of ten nonfiction books, a contributing author, co-editor, or coauthor of twelve others. She has also written three books in the fiction realm.

Linda has more than thirty years in the development field. She worked for a university and a museum before starting her consulting firm. In her twenty-five years as a philanthropic consultant, Linda has managed capital campaigns that have raised more than $50 million, helped hundreds of nonprofit organizations achieve their development goals, and trained more than forty thousand development professionals in most of the fifty states of the United States as well as Canada, Mexico, Egypt, and Bermuda.

She served on the Association of Fundraising Philanthropy (AFP) Foundation for Philanthropy Board and on the Professional Advancement Division for AFP. She is a past president of the Eastern Pennsylvania and Sierra (Nevada) AFP chapters. She received the Outstanding Fundraiser of the Year award from the Eastern Pennsylvania, Las Vegas, and Sierra (Nevada) chapters of AFP, was honored with the Barbara Marion Award for Outstanding Service to AFP, and received the Lifetime Achievement Award from the Las Vegas AFP chapter.

Linda is a graduate of Alvernia University with majors in banking and finance as well as theology/philosophy, and a minor in communications. As a graduate of AFP's Faculty Training Academy, she is a Master Teacher.

Dedication

This book is dedicated to all the executive directors, development directors, grant professionals, and volunteers who strive to bring in more resources in order to fulfill more mission.

Contents

Chapter One 1
What Foundation Reviewers Want to Know, Asked or Not

Chapter Two 5
What Need Will You Meet?

Chapter Three 11
How Will You Meet the Need You Describe?

Chapter Four 17
How Do You Know You Will Be Successful in Doing What You Say You Can Do?

Chapter Five 21
How Will You Measure Your Success?

Chapter Six 25
How Much Will Your Program Cost?

Chapter Seven 29
Do You Have Community Support?

Chapter Eight 33
How Will You Sustain Your Efforts?

Chapter Nine 37
What Makes You Uniquely Qualified to Do What You Say You Can Do?

Chapter Ten 41
Bringing It All Together

Chapter One

What Foundation Reviewers Want to Know, Asked or Not

Grant funding is a crucial part of many nonprofits' fundraising strategies. According to the Fundraising Effectiveness Project, foundations contribute 18 percent of all charitable giving. Foundations also tend to give bigger gift amounts than many individuals, often in the $5,000 to $100,000 range. That's a nice chunk of change if you can get it.

Foundation funding is getting harder and harder to get. According to the National Center for Charitable Statistics, there are more than 1.56 million nonprofits in the United States. Public charities, or 501(c)(3) organizations, make up about two-thirds of all nonprofits. Many of them are applying to the same foundations, competing with one another for funding. How do you make your organization stand out among the thousands of other nonprofits who have also applied to that particular foundation? What can you do as a grant professional to position your nonprofit as one of the best out there? What can you do to ensure a 'wow factor' is evident in your proposal when a reviewer assesses it? What can you do to secure your best chance of being funded?

The Questions Review Committees Want to be Answered

Have you ever written a grant proposal? What was your experience in writing it? Was it hard or easy? Was your request funded? Why or why not? Do you know so that you can repeat what worked and correct what didn't?

Writing a successful grant proposal is harder than it looks. Sometimes you are given detailed directions to follow; most times, you are not. Sometimes you are given a written structure for how to present concepts; often, you are not. Most often, you are given a page limit, sometimes even a word or character limit. It can be tough to present all the information you want to convey within these strict limits. Without a defined structure or with limited space, how do you know what information is most important to convey? How do you choose what to include and what to cut? What will help your proposal rise to the top when there are constraints or, conversely, little direction of what to include?

No matter what they ask for or how limited the space is for you to include it, there are eight crucial questions you must answer in every proposal you write. Answering these questions, no matter the format or space limitations, will ensure that your proposal is complete and propel it to the top of the pile.

The eight questions are:

1. What need will you meet?
2. How will you meet the need you describe?
3. How do you know you will be successful in doing what you say you can do?
4. How will you measure your success?
5. How much will your program cost?
6. Do you have community support?
7. How will you sustain your efforts?
8. What makes you uniquely qualified to do what you say you can do?

Answering all eight questions, whether asked in the application guidelines or not, will ensure your proposal stands out because you will have written a case for support that covers all the bases.

Review Committee Perspectives

Overwhelmingly, reviewers are looking for mission impact. They want to fund nonprofits that meet the community needs that their foundation is interested in impacting. They are most interested in what needs you want to meet, how you meet those needs, what kind of success you've had meeting them in the past, and what makes you think you'll be successful now.

You also have reviewers who are looking for something new, something beyond the same old things. Believe us, when you're looking at a hundred or more proposals, it's the unique ones that stand out. The agencies that know what makes them different than anyone else and can articulate it are the ones that make an impression. It's much easier to remember and be impressed by a nonprofit that knows its niche than one that is just like everyone else.

Then you have a reviewer or two who go straight to the budget and asks all kinds of questions about costs and if they're necessary and reasonable.

They look at the project and organizational budgets and attached agency financial statements and want to see financial strength and sound financial management.

You have other reviewers who are more interested in the nonprofit's reputation in the community and how well they work with others. These reviewers realize that the problems nonprofits address are big, hairy, and bodacious. They know that it takes a community to solve community-wide problems. These reviewers want to see how the nonprofit and their programs at hand fit into the community.

Generally, foundation funding is one-year funding. Foundations don't want to fund financial leeches. They want to make sure that the program being funded can exist beyond the foundation's limited funding, both during the term of the grant and after the grant has ended. They want to see that other partners have some sort of financial buy-in—that they are not just paying lip service to the program being considered. They want to see deep community collaborations.

Answering all eight questions, whether asked or not, helps address the multitude of concerns the foundation's board or review committee will have regarding funding your project. Showing awareness of all the concerns, and answering them, puts you in a favorable position when funding decisions are made.

Wrapping It Up

- There are more than 1.56 million nonprofits in the United States, many of them competing for the same pot of funding.
- To stand out, answer the eight questions, whether explicitly asked or not.
- Foundation reviewers are overwhelmingly looking for mission impact.
- Know your niche and be able to articulate it.
- Be able to show financial strength.
- Show your community connections.

Chapter Two

What Need Will You Meet?

Your needs statements are the crux of your proposal. The needs you choose to meet shape your proposal's stated goals, measurement of those goals, the program you implement to meet the goals, what accomplishments and community partnerships you highlight in the narrative, and what foundations to which you apply. To get the funding, you must get your needs section right. Because it determines how you approach so many other parts of the proposal, the needs section of the grant is the first section you should write.

Lack of Funding is Not a Need

Foundations do not give to nonprofits because they need money. Foundations are not ATM's dispensing money. Foundations are people making decisions about how they can best achieve impact. Foundations give money to nonprofits because they believe that, of all the applicants, the grant recipients will make the biggest, most sustainable, most financially responsible impact on solving the community problem outlined in their grant proposals. It is not money that makes an impact on a community problem. It is the way the money is used that makes an impact. And the way you use your money is encapsulated in your mission statement. Foundations give to fulfill a mission, not balance a checkbook. It is not the need for money that motivates foundations to give. It is the impact reached in improving the human condition that motivates foundations to give.

Also, positioning your nonprofit in need of money weakens your argument for funding. Who do you think review committees are going to fund: the applicants who can show financial strength, or the ones talking about their financial weakness? A financially strong applicant, of course. Lack of funding is not a need.

Lack of a Program is Not a Need

In a related vein, a lack of a program is not a need. Programs are organizational structures. Foundations want to impact people, not organizational structures. Organizational structures are in place to sustain organizational existence. Foundations are not interested in organizational sustenance. They are, however, interested in mission sustenance. The need you describe is related to the community and your organization's impact on it. It is not the program you implement that is important. What is important is how much impact on a community need your agency is making by implementing that particular program. When it comes to describing the need, it is not about starting or sustaining a program. The need is about the people you serve.

How to Determine True Need

The true need you describe in your proposal is about people and communities. What outcome is your nonprofit trying to achieve? What underlying need are you meeting? To get at true need, ask, "Why are we doing this?" until you can't anymore.

For example, why do you operate a food bank? Because people don't have money for food. Why is that important? Because people go hungry. And why is that important? One reason is that poor nutrition leads to chronic health problems. And chronic health problems require expensive health care interventions. And expensive health care interventions use more societal resources than operating a food bank. Because poor nutrition stunts growth and development is another reason why you don't want people to go hungry. Which leads to lower educational attainment. Which leads to lower-income jobs. Which can mean having to make choices between which living expenses to pay and not pay. Which may mean not having enough food to eat.

Notice the needs we are describing are not about the food bank. The food bank is the *program*. The needs we are describing are about the needs of individuals and the community: chronic health issues, the cost of health care, income instability, cyclical poverty. What has more impact on you: "We need a food bank in our community," or "Through a food bank, we can help people be healthier, attain income stability, decrease the societal costs of health care, and reduce poverty in our community"? Which statement do you think will make more of an impact on reviewers?

When you are describing a need in the community, you also need to address "why this particular community" as opposed to others—community meaning both the population you serve and the geographical area in which you operate. Why do you serve this specific population in this given area? Are they the poorest? Are they the sickest? Do they have the highest unemployment rate? Do they consume the most resources? Notice we are asking questions about the people we serve concerning the needs we have identified. When you describe why you are choosing to serve a particular segment of the community, make sure you explain that choice in relation to the primary needs you have identified. Remember, your proposal is probably one of hundreds. The reviewers are comparing your community's needs to the others they look at. Put your request in context for them. Make it easy for them to see how much community need there really is.

Documenting Needs in Your Narrative

When you write your needs statements, you can't just write them and expect reviewers to believe them just because you stated them. You need to base your needs statements on facts substantiated by respected authorities and leaders in the field. Sourcing your data gives credibility and lends weight to the importance of what you are saying.

Your needs section is the place where you give statistics, research findings, and outcome data. Governmental agencies are good sources of data. The U.S. Census Bureau is your best friend in gathering demographic data. The Center for Disease Control and Prevention is good for health and disease data. The Department of Housing and Urban Development has a plethora of housing and income data. The Family and Youth Services Bureau, part of the Administration for Children and Families, provides research findings on youth homelessness, adolescent pregnancy, and domestic violence. On a state level, your state's crime bureau will have arrest and crime data. Your state's education agency will have school and student test results data. The federal and state governments spend a lot of money on research, and they collect data on the many grants they administer. They are great resources for authoritative data.

Industry and professional groups are also well worth researching. For example, the Urban Institute is a good source for issues affecting urban areas, such as poverty, educational attainment, and employment data. The National Alliance to End Homelessness provides homelessness and affordable housing data. The Association on Intellectual and Developmental Disabilities is a good source for developmental disability data. The National Education Association and its state chapters may be good sources for student outcome data. The Chambers of Commerce sometimes have local business and economic data available through their sites. The Council for Nonprofits and its state affiliates share data on the welfare of nonprofits. In your search for widely accepted data, try researching the professional groups and associations relating to the industry or field of which your nonprofit is a part.

You can often find data through papers put out by foundations, too. For example, the Annie E. Casey Foundation publishes child welfare data. The Pew Charitable Trusts shares its research on contemporary political and civic issues. The Kresge Foundation publishes case studies on affordable housing. Gleaning information from the publications of the foundation you are applying to, if they have them, is a good strategy for presenting authoritative data.

Don't forget the objective, hands-on data you can glean from your own nonprofit's programs. There is nothing like having demographic data from the exact type of clients in the exact environments in which your grant programs will be implemented. Data like that tells the reviewers exactly what needs, strengths, and obstacles the population you serve experiences. If you have specific objective evidence of your constituencies' experiences in getting their needs met, by all means, use it. Especially if you can compare your agency's data to other authoritative data. Use whatever data you can to support the case for meeting the needs of your nonprofit's clients.

So, research, research, research. Get as much objective, authoritative, widely accepted data as you can.

Presenting Your Needs Data

When you present statistical data, make sure you do so in both actual numbers and percentages. You may round your numbers for easier reading, both the actual number and the percentages, but make sure you're consistent in your rounding method. You want context around your numbers. Remember, reviewers will probably be reading hundreds of proposals. You want the program your nonprofit operates to be able to be compared to other programs in other communities in which other nonprofits operate. Reviewers need both actual numbers and percentages to be able to put the programs in perspective from one organization to another and from one community to another. Having both numbers and percentages gives a more accurate picture of size and scope as opposed to using just one or the other.

Remember to source your statements. You want the foundation to know that credible authorities also see a need in your community. Don't just say what the statistic or research finding is. State the source of information.

And avoid the 'alphabet soup' for which nonprofits are famous. You may know what NEA, NIH, or FYSB mean, or whatever other acronyms you may commonly use, but chances are the reviewers don't. Reading through a proposal of 'alphabet soup' makes it hard to follow and difficult to read. That's not something you want your reviewers to feel. You want the reviewers to be able to understand readily the information you are presenting. So, avoid the alphabet soup.

The Importance of Matching Missions

The need your nonprofit meets is expressed in your organization's mission. The needs foundations want to meet are expressed in their missions. Your success in receiving funding from foundations is dependent upon your ability to match your nonprofit's mission with the foundations' missions. Don't apply to foundations where the two missions don't match. Only apply to foundations where their missions match yours. There is no sense in spending your time preparing applications that don't have a chance of being funded. Your time is too precious.

You also want to maintain your agency's reputation among the foundation community. Foundation funders are a pretty tight group. They are often members of the same professional organizations. Sometimes they have common board members. They sit on funding panels together. They do know each other. Information about individual nonprofits gets around. You do not want to be known as the nonprofit who doesn't do its homework. Maintain a good reputation. Do your homework. Match your nonprofit's mission to those of the foundations to which you apply.

Your needs statements shape the rest of your grant proposal. It is important that the needs section of your proposal's narrative talks about individual and community needs as opposed to organizational and financial needs. To spend your time effectively, match your agency's mission to the foundations you apply to.

Wrapping It Up
- Your needs statements are the crux of your grant proposal.
- The need you are meeting is about the individuals and community you serve, not the funding you need or the program you want to implement.
- Your underlying need is embedded in your mission statement. Ask, "Why do we do this?" until you can't anymore.
- Put your needs in context for the reviewers.

- Provide objective evidence that substantiates your statements.
- Match your nonprofit's mission to those of the foundations to which you apply.

Chapter Three

How Will You Meet the Need You Described?

Grant professionals often say the question, "How will you meet the need you described," is the easiest question for them to answer. And it usually is. A nonprofit usually has a pretty good handle on the programs they run. After all, you serve your constituency through the operation of programs. In fact, probably most of your organization's resources are spent administering services to clients. And probably most of those resources are human resources: paid or volunteer staff. With so many people involved in program delivery and so many resources invested in making sure programs run smoothly, it's no wonder that most nonprofits can accurately describe how they plan to meet their clients' needs.

Answering Why Your Agency Uses This Particular Program

Don't just dive in and start jotting down the who, what, where, when, and how of your program implementation. First, answer the question of why *this* program. Why do these specific staff do what they do when they do it and where they do it? For example, are you implementing an evidence-based program? Why? Because it's been shown to work among a group of people similar to the population you want to serve? If it's not formally evidence-based, why do you do what you do? What is the rationale behind your program operations? Is there some special circumstance you need to account for to deliver services among your group of clients or in your community effectively? Is that why you deliver services where you do? Is that why you offer services during the times you do? What about how you deliver services? Are there special characteristics about your client population such that services need to be delivered in a certain way? Or is there something about your overall agency programming that specifically meets the unique needs of your clients, for example, the complexity of their needs met or necessity for a one-stop shopping experience?

Your agency or program is unique. You have evidence that your programming works. You will use this information when you describe program operations. You will also use it in the narratives where you describe what makes your program or agency uniquely qualified to do what you say it will do—and where you project how you will know you will be successful in making the impact you wish to make. Of course, if you're serving a unique population group with unique needs, those needs will be highlighted in your needs statements. In your needs statements, you must mention all the needs your nonprofit wants to meet through this specific programming so that you have laid an objective rationale for why your agency is doing what it is doing in the way it is doing it.

Describing Your Program

This is where you answer the who, what, where, when, and how of the program. What is the goal of the program? Who, specifically, are you serving? What will you do to serve them? Who is providing program services? Do they have or need special training or credentials? Where are your programs providing services? Within what time frame? How do people find out about and enter your programs? What criteria must they meet when they complete the program? What tools or materials will you use to implement your program? What collaborations do you need to successfully implement for your program to work and successfully meet the total client needs?

You will not only want to describe the program in terms of the organizational journey; you will want to describe it through the eyes of a client. The clients' journey, from when they first become aware of your program to program exit, is important to illustrate. Not only does describing the client journey make operations come alive to the reviewer, but it will also illustrate exactly how client needs are met through that specific program implementation. The needs identified in your needs statements lay the basis for the methodology of your programs. The client journey gives a face to the statistics and research findings outlined in your needs statements.

You should also describe the process for how you will measure success. Program evaluation is crucial to program operations. Foundations want to know what impact their donation made on a community problem. What tools will your program use to know success was achieved? Surveys? Pre- and post-tests? Client interviews? Client observation? When will you implement them? How often? Where will you conduct evaluations? Who will do it? How? What happens after you finish conducting your evaluation? Program exit? Entrance into another agency program? Referral to another agency? Make sure you address the processes involved in measuring your program's success as part of your program operations narrative.

The best place to go for information to describe how a program works from beginning to end is a program manager or director. Go to someone who has experience in and understands how the program works at all organizational levels, from program marketing to final report and account closeout. You will also want to talk with someone who can explain the client journey from program awareness to program exit.

Be thorough, but be concise. Many grant professionals tend to go on too long about their nonprofits' programs because program services use up most of the agency resources and require the most amount of staff to implement. Most of the people in the organization are familiar with them. Even though this section of the narrative may be one of the longer sections, it is not the most important. There are eight equally important questions foundations want to be answered. Make sure you spend adequate time preparing a thorough answer for each question.

Stating Your Goals and Objectives

In the formal presentation of your proposal, the foundation will probably ask you to state your programs for goals and objectives. Foundations are interested in both the big, hairy, bodacious issues your nonprofit is trying to address as well as the impact that only a year's worth of limited funding will have.

Writing Goal Statements

Goal statements are based on the community needs identified in your needs statements. Your needs statements show what big, hairy, bodacious needs the people you serve face. The foundations you apply to are interested in addressing those same big, hairy, bodacious issues. Your goal statements name those issues and what you plan to do to influence them. In this way, your program's goals and the foundation's goals align with one another. Your goal statement lines up your program with the foundation's mission.

Your goals are the overall things you want to do. They are usually broadly defined and have long timeframes of a few to many years: reduce poverty, decrease pollution, eliminate homelessness, increase employment rates, improve self-esteem, raise health indices, to name a few. Whatever your goal, it is broad in nature and probably takes years from the time of program intervention to see significant results. For shorter proposals and smaller programs, you may only have one or two goal statements. For larger proposals, you may have several goal statements.

Your program's goals should always be a subset of your organizational goals. And your organizational goals should be based on your nonprofit's mission. If the program you want to implement does not relate to your nonprofit's mission, don't implement it. Don't even waste your time seeking funding for it. If you apply for funding and get it, you will be on your way to mission drift. Mission drift occurs when a nonprofit's resources are used for things other than mission. Once mission drift begins, your organizational identity starts to change. If it continues, people will sooner or later not know what your agency stands for, and you will lose community support. Not only in terms of your foundation donors but your individual and business ones too. Foundations will not fund you because your organization is not meeting its stated mission. Individuals will question how their donations will be used. Businesses will see your agency's weak identity and not want to partner with you. Remember, apply to foundations where your mission and their mission matches. Foundations are after mission impact. They like to fund nonprofits who meet their defined missions.

Writing Objectives

Objectives, as opposed to your broad goal statements, are specific, measurable, action-oriented, realistic, and time-bound, often referred to as SMART. You will most likely have two or more objectives for each goal. Objectives are usually formulated in yearlong increments. For example, five hundred eleventh-grade students will learn how to write essays through the We Can Succeed as Writers writing program as measured by a score of ninety-five or above on the eleventh-grade state writing aptitude test. Notice we quantified our outcomes in terms of population served, the number of people we want to serve, the mechanism we will use to serve them, the time frame in which they will receive services, and how we plan to measure the effect of the intervention. Grant professionals constantly ask what magic numbers foundations want to see in their applicants' grant objectives. The answer is, what is realistic for your organization. Your organization's program staff—those on the front lines of working with clients—know best what is achievable. Make sure you have program input when you articulate your objectives.

When you ask your program staff for input, ask about capacity and timeframes. We have seen more than one nonprofit fail to meet its grant objectives, risking their reputation within the foundation community, because they overpromised the amount of service they could deliver. Or, the nonprofit met its objectives but spent much more money doing it than the grant funding provided. The nonprofit lost money, and the program staff resented the grant professional for the extra work required. Yes, the nonprofit got the grant funding. But the costs outweighed the benefits.

Most nonprofits intimately understand their program operations. In fact, most of their staff and resources are probably directed toward service delivery. Tap into those resources when gathering program information. Ask program staff questions that will help you formulate SMART objectives. Have program directors describe program operations at all levels of the organization. Talk to frontline staff about the client journey. Let the reviewers experience your program through your client journey description. Match your agency's program's goals to the foundation's goals. Your program's goals should relate to your nonprofit's mission. If they don't, the costs of funding will far outweigh the benefits. Although your program narrative may be lengthy, remember it is still only one question out of eight that foundations want to be answered.

Wrapping It Up

- Answer the question of why this *specific* program is the best alternative to meet your clients' needs.
- Describe program operations at all levels of the organization.
- Describing the client journey puts a face to your operations.
- Be thorough but concise.
- Goal statements are broad. The period between program intervention and significantly achieving a goal is usually measured over years.
- Good objectives are specific, measurable, action-oriented, realistic, and time-bound.

Chapter Four

How Do You Know You Will Be Successful in Doing What You say You Can Do?

Answering how you know you will be successful in doing what you say you can do is trickier than it sounds. Many grant professionals only project the success of their agency's program implementation. But, as we have seen, it is not how well we implement organizational structures that foundations are interested in. Foundations are interested in mission impact. So, if it's not your program assessing, how do you project success?

Measuring Goals and Objectives

Your project demonstrates success by how well your nonprofit will reach its goals and objectives, not how well it implements its programs. Remember, programs are organizational structures. Reviewers don't care about organizational structures. They care about the impact. They are interested in what impact will be made in the community through their donation. They want to know what impact their money makes in solving a community issue. Your organization's program is only a conduit for them to reach their missions. So, remember to talk about mission and goals when touting your organization's success. Make the foundation the hero in the impact your nonprofit will make as a result of its grant. If you matched missions and based your goals on your needs statements, this will be easy because your program will already be lined up with the foundation's mission.

Of course, the big, hairy, bodacious issues your nonprofit is addressing will probably take years to show improvement significantly. Your goal statements are broad and not easily measurable within a year's worth of funding. To show improvement over a year, you measure your objectives. If you've written SMART objectives, it's easy to measure them. Let's take the last chapter's example objective of five hundred eleventh-grade students learning how to write essays through the We Can Succeed as Writers writing program as measured by a score of ninety-five or above on the eleventh-grade state writing aptitude test. When we talk about how we want to evaluate whether we've succeeded, we just ask whether five hundred eleventh-grade students who went through the We Can Succeed as Writers program scored ninety-five or higher on the state writing aptitude test.

Writing about how you measure your success is simple if you've written good goals and objectives. We often find the evaluation sections of our grant proposals the easiest to write.

Articulating Historical Success

Another way to project success is through history. The history piece is usually the organizational background and description section of your proposal, also called the credibility statement. The best predictor of future success is past results. What are your nonprofit's past results? Is your agency an old pro at doing what it says it can do? What results has your program achieved? How is that program similar to the one you are proposing? What infrastructure is already built that will help your organization achieve your program's desired results?

What about people outside your organization? What do clients say about your program? What about service partners and agency collaborators? What have funders said? What have evaluators said? Did they say anything about your program or whole organization? Is your nonprofit known for being the best at something? What is it? Who says so? If you've been successful at something before, chances are you will be successful at that again.

The history doesn't have to be something your organization or program has done. You can also be replicating others' successful programs, like evidence-based programs. Evidence-based programs have been validated to work in the studied populations through objective, third-party research. To become evidence-based, these programs are applicable across a wide spectrum of clients and communities. If you are going to be using an evidence-based program in your interventions with clients, make sure you cite the evidence-based research findings. That research will give your program tons of credibility and assurance that your program will most likely meet its goals.

Using Comparative Data

Another way to show success is to use comparative data. If you have data you've collected from your program clients, you can compare results over time. If you serve clients for long periods, you can show improvement before and after the intervention. If you serve different client groups at different times, you can show repeated success over time. You can also compare your clients' outcomes to national, state, or local averages. If your outcomes are better than average, you have a strong argument for success. Also, you can compare your clients' outcomes to client outcomes of similar programs in similar communities. If you are implementing a program new to your organization, you can compare outcomes of similar population groups or communities who have utilized your program choice to your organization's client population group or community. If the population groups or communities are similar, logic dictates that success in one group is transferrable to a similar group.

Your evaluation section is where you measure your nonprofit's success in meeting its goals and objectives. However, success can be addressed in other sections of your grant proposal as well. Your organizational history should demonstrate your agency's success. Citing evidence-based programs in describing your program is also often used to anticipate success. In addition, comparative data can be effectively used to predict success.

Wrapping It Up
- Goals may take years to measure significant impact.
- Evaluating your program objectives is simple if you've written SMART objectives.
- The best predictor of future success is past results. Use historical data to anticipate program success.
- Comparative data can also be used to forecast success effectively.

Chapter Five

How Will You Measure Your Success?

In **Chapter Four,** we talked about projecting success. In this chapter, we turn our attention to the different ways on which we can base success.

Basing Success on Mission Consistency

One basis of success is how consistently your agency fulfills its mission throughout organizational operations. The goal is to present a strong front of unified resources directed toward one thing: fulfilling mission. The way to show organizational resources are unified is to show a consistency of purpose and values throughout the agency.

The easiest way to show consistency throughout an agency is through strict adherence to organizational policies and procedures. Policy is generally set and enforced by the board. Procedures are generally set and enforced by management. Board policies ensure that the nonprofit's leadership obtains and allocates community resources toward mission fulfillment. Well-formulated policies promote strict adherence to agency mission, vision, and values. Well-formulated procedures ensure consistent adherence to policy, that is, adherence to its mission, vision, and values, throughout agency operations.

This is why funders sometimes directly ask about an applicant's policies and procedures. They are trying to determine a nonprofit's consistency in fulfilling its mission throughout the organization. They want to make sure the resources they may contribute will be used for mission fulfillment. They are, after all, doing the same thing you are—matching missions. Just as you look for foundations whose missions match yours, so do foundations look for agencies whose missions match theirs.

At the very least, make sure to mention your nonprofit's values and vision statements in your grant proposal, probably in the agency description and background section. You may also want to add descriptive phrases that relate to your mission, vision, or values when you describe your program. For example, if your mission is to encourage civic participation, then you might start your objectives section with the phrase, "To promote greater civic participation, we will..." If one of your nonprofit's values is equality, you might qualify your program methods by saying, "We will ensure people are treated equally by..."

Be consistent even in your budget, other funding, and sustainability sections. For example, if your goal is livable wages for your clients, does your agency provide livable wages to its employees? Or, just how does that Casino Night fundraising event promote your agency's mission?

Make sure all the elements of your proposal are consistent with your nonprofit's mission, vision, and values.

Basing Success on Meeting the Goals and Objectives of Your Agency's Strategic Plan

Another easy way to show success is to describe how well your agency is meeting the goals and objectives of its strategic plan. A strategic plan is a road map showing how your nonprofit will fulfill its mission into the future. Having a strategic plan anticipates your nonprofit's success in fulfilling mission in the years to come. Past success shows your agency can set and reach goals. A brief mention of what goals have been met in the past portrays an organization that has fulfilled its mission in the past. As we saw in **Chapter Four**, the best predictor of future success is past results.

Successful implementation of a strategic plan also shows that your nonprofit is chasing mission fulfillment as opposed to financial gain. Nonprofits who chase money rather than mission are open to mission drift. Mission drift occurs when agency resources are used in pursuit of things other than mission. If mission drift occurs, sooner or later your agency will lose community support, as we saw in **Chapter Two**. Adherence to a strategic plan bolsters your grant request by subtly showing lack of funding is not your need.

According to the Concord Leadership Group, only about half of nonprofits have a strategic plan. Hopefully, your nonprofit has a strategic plan that is updated annually.

Basing Success on Meeting Standards and Practices in the Field

Still another easy way to show success is to state how your nonprofit meets or exceeds widely accepted standards in your field. Know the standards in your field and show how your agency compares to industry benchmarks. You should mention your agency's competence in meeting or exceeding industry standards in the background and description section of your proposal.

Similarly, your proposal should show how your agency implements widely accepted practices in the field. Showing the use of best practices highlights your agency as the cream of the crop, one of the best out there. Mention widely accepted industry and best practices when you write about how your agency will carry out its program activities.

Basing Success on Your Proposal's Evaluation Mechanisms

We talked about measuring your goals and objectives in **Chapter Four**. Presenting past positive client outcomes before and after the intervention and over time can be powerful predictors of success.

To further illustrate organizational success, you may also want to present the progress your program makes in meeting its operational milestones. For example, for clients to exit the program, they need to enter the program. What program recruitment strategies did you describe? How successful are your client recruitment methods? What about program retention? How successful is your program in retaining clients? What are your program participation rates? How many clients successfully exit the program? The more objective data you have, the more you will be able to substantiate the success of your program interventions.

Presenting Your Evaluation Data

Just as we talked about in **Chapter Two** when you quantify needs, when you present statistical forecasts in your evaluation statements, do so in both actual numbers and percentages. Make sure the rounding method in your evaluation section is consistent with that of your needs statements. Remember that reviewers will probably be reading hundreds of proposals. You want the impact your program makes to be comparable to other programs in other proposals. Having both the actual numbers as well as the percentages helps the reviewer measure impact from one program to another.

Basing success on mission fulfillment can be powerful. Make sure organizational adherence to your nonprofit's mission, vision, and values is consistent throughout all elements of your proposal. Having a strategic plan anticipates future existence. Illustrating success in implementing your strategic plan gives credibility to your organization's ability to set goals and meet them in the future. You can easily measure success by comparing your agency's performance to industry benchmarks and widely accepted practices in the field. When you present statistical evaluation information, do it in a format consistent with your needs statements.

Wrapping It Up

- Be consistent in illustrating your nonprofit's mission, vision, and values across all elements of your proposal.
- Use adherence to your organization's strategic plan to substantiate your agency's credibility.
- Compare your nonprofit's performance to industry benchmarks and widely accepted practices in the field.
- In addition to client outcomes, show your agency's success in achieving operational milestones.
- Make sure you format numbers consistently throughout your proposal.

Chapter Six

How Much Will Your Program Cost?

Crafting a budget is often the least-liked, most-feared part of writing a grant proposal. Yet, as we saw in **Chapter One**, there are plenty of grant reviewers who are first and foremost concerned about your program's budget. They would rather review a page of revenue and expense projections than read pages and pages of text. They understand that your grant proposal's budget is a one-page financial representation of your narrative. Through the budget, they can see what amount of funding your nonprofit is asking, how those funds will be used, whether your costs are reasonable or not, what other financial resources are needed, and how much community support there is behind the project. A well-written budget can also tell reviewers about the scope of your intervention. That's a lot of information on one page. You must get the budget right.

Creating Your Grant Budget with the Input of the Program Director

The easiest way to develop your grant budget is to create it alongside your narrative. Make two columns. Label one column "Expenses" and the other "Revenues."

Then talk to your agency's program staff, the ones who will be implementing the grant. As we discussed in **Chapter Three**, information about how a program works is best gathered from a program director who understands how the program works at all organizational levels.

As you are gathering information, whenever that director tells you what tasks staff members do, how many staff members do it at a time, how many hours it takes each staff member to do, and how many weeks a year each staff member will be doing it, write that information down under "Expenses." When the program director tells you about something provided to clients—transportation, food, rent, school supplies, sports equipment, musical instruments, to name a few—write those things down under "Expenses." Whatever outside consultants help design, deliver, or evaluate your program, write them down under "Expenses." Whatever conferences or trainings program staff will attend, write down how many will attend at what conference under "Expenses." How staff will be getting from the office to where service delivery or training will take place, jot it down under "Expenses." Write down everything it takes to operate the program successfully. You want your budget to be as detailed as your narrative. If you discover expenses that you have not included in the narrative, go back and talk about them in the narrative.

If funding other than the foundation's will be used in implementing the program, the name of those funders goes under "Revenues." Whatever it is that community partners contribute to program functioning, write that down. Other foundations, businesses, and government agency donors should each have a line in the budget and be listed under "Revenues." Whenever the program director talks about donations given to the program, write those down under "Revenues." If the program is using space for free, write that down under "Revenues." If your program charges client fees, write those down under "Revenues." If your organization will be raising funds for the program, write those down under "Revenues." Give each community partner its own revenue line. Make sure the community partners listed in your budget are talked about in your narrative.

Congratulations! You have just developed the majority of your budget lines. In other words, you have just created a large portion of your budget. Now the task is to develop the rest of your budget lines and put numbers to them.

Creating Your Grant Budget with Input from the Finance Officer

The best person to go to for the rest of your budget lines is your finance officer. Your finance officer will have your agency's chart of accounts. A chart of accounts is a list of all your organization's revenue and expense lines. Your finance officer will be able to tell you what line items you need to add to your budget for the program to be viable, and your organization not lose money. Yes, it *is* possible for the grant to be funded and your nonprofit to lose money still. Your nonprofit will lose money on the funded project if the expenses exceed the revenues. The only way to make sure all the expenses are covered is to include them in the budget. And it is your finance officer who can compare your grant budget to the agency chart of accounts and add what lines are missing.

For example, your finance offer can add the fringe benefits the agency pays employees. Fringe benefits are usually expressed as a percentage of salary. Sometimes funders want the total percentage of all the fringe benefits, and sometimes they want them spelled out.

Your finance officer can also add in the core organizational costs the agency must pay. Finance, technology, human resources, fundraising, executive management, board development, and marketing are necessary core organizational operations. Your finance director will be able to add those core line items to your budget. Sometimes these expenses are listed individually, and sometimes they are grouped as General and Administrative (G&A). G&A is usually expressed as a percentage of total program costs.

Now give a dollar value to all the line items.

Your finance officer will have salary information. If you know how many hours a week and how many weeks a year the program staff is involved in carrying out your program, your finance officer can figure what percentage of their time can be allocated to the grant. Add in fringe benefits, and you have the personnel section of your budget done. Make sure your line item text has enough detail such that the calculation leading to the line item amount is obvious.

Except for G&A, the rest of your expenses are classified as nonpersonnel expenses. Note that consultants are included in the nonpersonnel expenses part of your expense budget. The agency does not provide fringe benefits to consultants; therefore, consultants are not included under personnel. The finance officer may provide some, but not all, of the nonpersonnel expenses. You may have to do some pricing research, especially if you are proposing a new program that will entail new lines in the chart of accounts.

If the foundation allows G&A, add up your personnel and nonpersonnel expenses. Take the total, multiply it with your G&A percentage, and add in your nonprofit's G&A. List your individual expenses, one per line. Then take your individual expenses lines and add them all up for the amount of total expenses. You now have a complete expense budget.

Now, list your individual revenue sources, one per line, and add them to show total revenue. The difference between how much revenue is coming in and how many expenses you will have to pay is the amount of funds you still need, either through fundraising or other revenue sources.

Revenue should always equal expenses. You want to show that the amount you are asking the foundation for is the exact amount you need.

If your revenues are greater than your expenses, then you don't need the money. Take one of your revenue sources and use it for another agency program. If your revenues are less than your expenses, you don't have enough to operate the program and stay solvent. You and your team have more fundraising to do.

Before submitting the budget to the foundation, check the numbers. Make sure your addition and multiplication are correct. Make sure the numbers in your budget match the numbers in your narrative. Check and double-check. Mathematical errors and financial inconsistencies are two of the most common mistakes a reviewer sees. Not only are these errors irritating, but they can also be confusing. Which facts are correct—the ones in your narrative or the ones in your budget?

Stating Your Request

You should always make a direct request for funding in your narrative. Be direct and brief. The request section of your proposal will be the shortest. Say something like, "[Name of my nonprofit] would like to partner with ABC Foundation in [program goal]. We are asking $X from the ABC Foundation.

If you have other sources of funding, show that too. Say something like, "The total cost of this project is $Y. DEF Foundation, GHI Foundation, and JKL Corporation are contributing a total of $Z to this project. [Name of your nonprofit] is also contributing to this project through (fees, gifts in kind, volunteers, etc.)."

Your proposal's budget is a financial representation of your narrative. Develop your budget with both the program director and finance officer. Once you have a complete budget, check your math. Make sure all the line items mentioned in your budget are mentioned in your narrative and that all resources needed for successful program implementation are included in your budget. Also, make sure the numbers stated in your budget are consistent with those in the narrative.

Wrapping It Up

- Your budget is a financial representation of your narrative. Make sure they are consistent with one another.
- Develop your budget with input from both program and finance staff.
- Make sure your line item text fully explains the calculation behind the line item amount.
- Check your math.
- Be brief in stating a direct request for funding.

Chapter Seven

Do You Have Community Support?

Community support is crucial to nonprofit survival. After all, nonprofits are governed by community leaders to meet community needs with the majority of their support coming from community individuals and organizations. Even if the foundation you are applying to will be the sole program funder, you will still need to show broad community support. Foundations today realize that tackling big, hairy, bodacious community issues requires a big, hairy, bodacious community effort. No one organization can do it on its own. The problems are just too big.

Showing Community Support through Agency Partnerships

Most grant professionals intuitively know that showing community support is about articulating partnerships. However, some of these partnerships are more visible than others. Formal partnerships are usually obvious. Informal partnerships may be less apparent.

Formal partnerships are usually solidified in writing, such as a contract or memorandum of understanding. They include agreements for running joint programs, sharing joint space, conducting joint studies, providing monetary and nonmonetary donations, licensing and accrediting programs, and sharing industry information. Formal partnerships can encompass organizational operations, client recruitment, service delivery, program evaluation, financial support, and access to industry information, among others. Sometimes money exchanges hands, sometimes not. When you identify your formal community partners, it doesn't matter if money is exchanged. In fact, most of the time, no money may be involved. Government contracts, licensing and accreditation agencies, association memberships, and agency donors are a few often-overlooked nonprofit formal partnerships.

Informal partnerships are harder to recognize but are still very important. Even a small agency without any formal partnerships can show community support. How? Board membership representation. How large is your board? What segments of your community do they represent? With what community groups are they involved?

In the same vein, staff representation can be used to show community support. How big is your nonprofit's staff? What communities do they live in? What segment of the community do they represent? What community groups are they involved with?

What about your volunteers? Volunteers are a great way to show community support. They donate time and labor to your programs. How big is your volunteer base? From where do they come? Who do they represent? You should always highlight volunteer involvement in your grant proposals.

Showing Community Support through Agency Community Participation

In addition to formal and partnerships, the actual work of your nonprofit can be used to show community support. What community input shapes the work of your nonprofit? For example, in what community meetings or task forces does your executive director or other staff participate? What community plans did the public contribute to and is your agency a part of? In what community surveys were your nonprofit's services mentioned or did your organization complete? What industry standards and practices are widely accepted in the community? Adherence to industry standards and practices implies community support.

In addition, your research into writing your grant proposals can imply community support. What community resources are you using to substantiate community need? Just by sourcing your needs statements, you are showing community involvement in studying the needs your nonprofit meets. By articulating good needs statements in your proposal, you are showing a community involvement, because community needs are emphasized as opposed to financial or program foci. Even your client base can show community support. After all, your clients are from the community.

Showing Community Support in Your Budget, Monetary Request, and Financial Sustainability Statements

As we saw in **Chapter Six**, your budget is a monetary reflection of your narrative. What formal and informal partnerships generate revenue for your nonprofit that can be used to support the program in question? Are any of your partners donating space, goods, or services to your agency or clients? What other foundations are contributing to your program?

What corporate entities are sponsoring the program? How many dollars are individuals contributing to the program? How many dollars are your clients contributing to your program through service fees? Don't overlook the power of your budget and direct request for funding to show strong community support.

Formal partnerships are often more obvious than informal ones. Both can be used to illustrate broad community support. Formal partnerships are usually solidified in writing and may or may not involve an exchange of money. Board, staff, and volunteer community involvement can demonstrate community support. The work of your agency, and even of your grant writing, can express community support. Use your revenue budget to provide financial evidence of broad community support.

Wrapping It Up

- Formal agency partnerships illustrate community support, including those in which money is exchanged.
- Board, staff, and volunteer community affiliations exhibit community support.
- The work of your agency, methods described your programming, and research cited in your needs statement all imply community support.
- Your revenue budget and funding request can be powerful tools in demonstrating strong community support.

Chapter Eight

How Will You Sustain Your Efforts?

As we stated in **Chapter One**, funders do not want leeches. They want to know what you are going to do when their funding runs out. Foundations generally want their contributions to make more than a year's worth of impact. They are looking to make a significant impact over a long period. How do you show sustainability, especially if you are a small nonprofit with limited resources?

Demonstrating Financial Sustainability

Financial sustainability is demonstrated through good financial planning. Good financial planning is accomplished through good financial management, solid revenue generation, and protection of assets. A well-written strategic plan addresses all three of these areas. The 50 percent of nonprofits with a written strategic plan are ahead of the game. Their chances of succeeding in an environment of increasing demands with decreasing resources are far better than those nonprofits with no written plan. This is why foundations ask about strategic plans. They know the strength that results from the strategic planning process. We talked about using the strategic plan as a basis for success in your proposal narrative in **Chapter Five**.

The way to demonstrate good financial management in your grant proposal is to include a brief statement of your agency's financial procedures. In most cases, due to length restrictions, you'll need to get it down to a sentence or two. In longer proposals, usually, when requesting large sums of money, foundations may ask for more detailed information.

Good financial management also means having reserves for a rainy day. How many months of operations can your reserves fund? The recommended amount is three to six months. If you don't have that much, how will you get it? What will you do if you experience an unexpected expense that must be paid? Tell the foundation your plans for dealing with financial emergencies.

To demonstrate solid revenue generation, include all sources of revenue in your sustainability plans. For example, if your organization has an endowment, state how much in interest or dividends is going to be used for program operations, if any. If your nonprofit realizes fees from goods or services, state your agency's plans for continuing or increasing the earned income stream. Talk about your fundraising efforts through individual donations, business contributions, government contracts, and special events, as well as other foundations. Just how do you plan to continue to raise the revenues you included in your revenue budget?

Let the foundation know you will protect the resources your nonprofit so painstakingly obtained. What are the checks and balances in your organization's accounting systems? How do you care for your agency's facilities and equipment? What about your nonprofit's confidential client, employee, donor, and financial information? Is there other property your organization needs to protect? An often-overlooked one is intellectual property.

Mentioning assets in your sustainability section is evidence of financial strength. Assets are a measure of wealth. They are resources that are quantified in your nonprofit's financial statements. Possession of long-term assets means some resources will last sometime into the future. Developing and maintaining assets is an essential part of any nonprofit's financial strategy.

Demonstrating Program Sustainability

In addition to financial sustainability, you should address program sustainability in your grant narrative. By program sustainability, I am referring to how your organization will sustain its operations. For example, how does your nonprofit attract and recruit staff, especially in a tight labor market? What retention strategies does your organization employ to keep talented staff? What about the space your program uses? Does your agency own or rent space? If your nonprofit rents, how long is the agreement? If space is donated, how long will that agreement last?

You also need to mention program sustainability in terms of program clients. How do potential clients become aware of your program? How does your nonprofit fill openings in your programs? How long does it take? Do you accept referrals into your programs? From whom? What is the process? In other words, how do you market your program, and what is your clients' initial experience? We talked about the client journey in **Chapter Three**.

Rather than sentences, answer most questions about program sustainability by adding descriptive adjectives and adverbs, and adjective and adverbial phrases, to sentences in sections other than the sustainability section. The section where you describe your program's operations is ideal. Space is limited in most foundation proposals. You may need to figure out ways to be extremely concise. Some proposals have word limits. Some even have character limits.

Demonstrating Mission Sustainability

In addition to financial and program sustainability, address mission sustainability in your grant narrative. This is most easily done by referencing your nonprofit's strategic plan. We talked about measuring success through an agency strategic plan in **Chapter Five**. A strategic plan is a written road map of how your agency plans on fulfilling its mission. Having a strategic plan anticipates future existence. Following the strategy outlined in the strategic plan assumes mission sustainability. Needing to update the plan regularly means that your organization has met its goals and objectives or that it is responding to some sort of change. Both indicate mission sustainability and organizational strength.

Financial stability is what most grant professionals write about in the sustainability sections of their proposals. To demonstrate financial sustainability, show good financial management, solid revenue generation, and adequate asset protection. To cover all your bases, address program and mission sustainability in addition to financial sustainability. Talk about program operations and marketing when addressing program sustainability. Reference your nonprofit's strategic plan to address mission sustainability. You may need to find creative ways to communicate mission and program sustainability concisely.

Wrapping It Up

- In your proposal, address financial, program, and mission sustainability.
- Financial sustainability is demonstrated through good financial management, solid revenue generation, and adequate asset protection.
- Describing how your program will sustain its operations is just as important as describing how it will sustain its finances.
- Regular strategic planning is a good indicator of mission sustainability.

- Be creative and concise in communicating sustainability to adhere to the foundation's page, word, or character limitations.

Chapter Nine

What Makes You Uniquely Qualified to Do What You Say You Can Do?

To get the competitive grant funding, your proposal must stand out from all the others in some way. You need to describe your organization's uniqueness. Your nonprofit may be unique in its history, program management and implementation, financial position, or leadership. Since only half of nonprofits have one, having a written strategic plan also sets your agency apart. Also, your proposal itself can set your nonprofit apart.

Highlighting Your Nonprofit's Past and Present Efforts

Your agency's history can demonstrate uniqueness. When was your nonprofit founded? Why was it founded? How long has it been in existence? How many people have you served during that time? What impact has your organization had on the issue you were founded to affect? What societal crises has your nonprofit faced? What did your agency do to prepare for them? How did your organization deal with them? What events in your nonprofit's history are unique? What has your agency done that no other organization has done?

Don't only point out what your nonprofit has done in the past. Write about present uniqueness, too. Is your organization the one and only of its kind in the community? Is your agency a leader in the community? If so, what leadership positions does your agency's leadership hold in the community? Is your nonprofit a leader in your field? What research efforts is your organization sponsoring or spearheading? What honors, awards, licenses, certifications, or accreditations does your agency enjoy?

Is the program you describe in your proposal unique in your community? What does your program do that no other does? Does your program serve a unique population? Is the scope of intervention broader or more comprehensive than other programs? Is the cost of the intervention lower than other programs? What are the program's past results? Are the outcomes better or more long-lasting than other programs? What evidence can you reference to prove your claims?

We raised most of these questions in previous chapters. A foundation will probably not ask you outright about what makes your nonprofit unique. Instead, you will be weaving your agency's or program's uniqueness in your proposal's background and organization description sections, as we talked about in **Chapters Four** and **Five**, and your program operations section, as we talked about in **Chapter Three**.

Highlighting Your Nonprofit's Management and Leadership

In addition to the uniqueness of your agency's past and present, your nonprofit's financial position may be unique. For example, if your agency is not experiencing the same threats as those in your community or industry, highlight why. If you have an endowment, emergency reserves, or several months of operating reserves, say it. Most probably, you will talk about how your agency has handled or is handling threats in your field or community in your organizational background and description sections. Your financial strength, as we talked about in **Chapter Eight**, can be addressed in your sustainability section.

Make sure whatever financial position you highlight is consistent with the financial picture your audit and IRS Form 990 paints. Even if you aren't asked to submit it, your nonprofit's 990 can be found on GuideStar at *https://www.guidestar.org*.

Your nonprofit's leadership team may also be unique. How diverse are your board membership and staff composition? Does the board or staff participate in advanced trainings above what is common in the field? Do any of your staff hold advanced degrees or certifications? Have any board or staff members been bestowed with any honors or awards in their fields? In addition to highlighting organizational and program uniqueness, talk about what sets your board and staff apart.

As in describing your organization's and program's uniqueness, you will likely be weaving your board and staff members' credentials in your proposal's background and organization description sections and your program operations section. You will probably be using descriptive adjectives and phrases, as opposed to stand-alone paragraphs, although some foundations do ask for key staff duties and credentials. Another good place to highlight staff credentials is through their resumes, if asked for. If a foundation does ask for resumes, make sure the resumes are clean and up to date. You may have to rewrite the resumes.

If your agency has a written strategic plan, your organization already stands out in the field. As we saw in **Chapter Five**, only about half of nonprofits have a written strategic plan. Having a written strategic plan is correlated to future success. Sometimes a reference to the strategic plan is a phrase at the beginning of a sentence alluding to the fact that the program you are proposing is part of a larger vision. If your organization has a strategic plan, referencing it even briefly will set you apart.

Proofreading Your Proposal

An often-overlooked way to set your organization apart is through the presentation of the proposal itself, that is, how it physically looks. For example, is the cover letter addressed to the right contact, to the right foundation, with the right address? Are all the names spelled correctly? Reviewers often get proposals that contain incorrect contact information. If the nonprofit can't manage to get the contact information right, how in the world will it manage the foundation's funding? Before submission, check to make sure the proposal is addressed correctly.

Sometimes, to gain space, grant writers decrease margins or font size. Don't do this. It just makes your proposal look crowded. If you run out of space because of the foundation's page, word, or character limits, work on being concise in your wording as opposed to making margins or font sizes smaller. You want plenty of white space on each page. You want your proposal to look pleasing and be easy on the eyes. You want your proposal to be as readable as you can make it. If you were reading through a hundred proposals, which is more appealing to you? The crowded, text-heavy one or the one that is laid out nicely with adequate white space?

Typos, misspellings, and grammatical errors are also common. They interrupt the thought flow and make reading difficult. They also show poor attention to detail. Use spell- and grammar-checking software. Proofread your proposal. Proofread it again. Do whatever you need to do to avoid typos, misspellings, and grammatical errors.

Throughout your proposal, weave in what makes your nonprofit unique. Highlight your agency's one-of-a-kind past and present. Talk about unique aspects of your program intervention. Write about how your agency has faced past crises and is prepared to face future ones. Feature board and staff credentials. Reference your nonprofit's strategic plan, if you have one. Present your proposal so that it is easily readable and pleasing to the eye. Present your agency as the cream of the crop through your layout.

Wrapping It Up

- Write about your nonprofit's unique past and present.
- Point out the uniqueness of your program intervention.
- Show financial strengths that paint the same picture as your agency's audit and 990.
- Highlight board and staff attainment.
- Reference your strategic plan.
- Submit a clean proposal.

Chapter Ten

Bringing It All Together

There are more than 1.56 million nonprofits in the United States, many of them competing for the same funding. How can your proposal stand out from the rest? To stand out, answer the eight questions we've talked about in this book, whether the foundation directly asks them or not.

When you format the proposal information for final grant submission, use the funder's format, if given. You want the reviewer to be able to find the information important to them easily. Find a way to include answers to all eight questions within the given format. Remember, you may need to condense information down to an adjective or adverb or an adjective or adverbial phrase. Make your narrative thorough but concise. Proofread your application. Submit a clean proposal.

When you are asked for background or descriptive information about your organization, include information on what makes your nonprofit uniquely qualified to do what you say it can do. Write about your agency's unique past and present. Use historical data to anticipate program success. Compare your nonprofit's performance to industry benchmarks and widely accepted practices in the field. Point out the uniqueness of your program intervention. Reference your agency's strategic plan. Use adherence to your organization's strategic plan to substantiate your agency's credibility. Highlight board and staff attainment. Mention your organization's financial strengths. Talk about formal and informal agency partnerships, including board, staff, and volunteer community affiliations.

Your needs assessment is the crux of your proposal. The needs you are meeting are about the individuals and community you serve, not the funding you're requesting or the program your nonprofit wants to implement. Provide objective evidence that substantiates your needs statements. Put your needs in context for the reviewers by using comparative data.

Your goals should match the goals of the foundation to which you are applying. Your goals articulate the big, hairy, bodacious issues your program is addressing. Goal statements are broad. It usually takes years to meet expressed goals.

Your objectives are the steps you will employ to meet your goals. Good objectives are SMART: specific, measurable, action-oriented, realistic, and time-bound. Writing SMART objectives makes articulating your evaluation measures easy.

When asked to describe your program, use as much detail as you can. The details will be used to create your budget line items. Describe program operations at all levels of your organization. In addition to answering the question of how the program works, answer the question of why this specific program is the best choice to meet your clients' needs. Also, describe the client experience. Describing the client journey puts a human face to your operations.

Base your anticipated outcomes on your stated objectives. When you are asked to evaluate your program's success, talk about progress made toward meeting your objectives as well as how well your program operations ran. Show client outcomes as well as your nonprofit's success in achieving program milestones.

Your budget is a financial representation of your narrative. Make sure your budgets and narrative are consistent with one another. Develop your budget with input from both program and finance staff. Explain your individual line item amounts in your line item text. Make sure your budget calculations are consistent with how your narrative says those resources are allocated.

In addition to financial data, your budget can be a tool to show strong community support. Check and double-check your math. Math errors are irritating and can be confusing to reviewers.

Make a direct ask for a specific amount of funding. Be brief. In addition to asking for the foundation's contribution, tell the reviewers how much money has already been raised and who else is contributing to the project.

When asked about how your nonprofit will sustain its efforts, address financial, program, and mission sustainability. Financial sustainability is demonstrated through good financial management, solid revenue generation, and adequate asset protection. Describing how your agency will sustain its program operations is just as critical as describing how it will sustain its finances. Articulating mission sustainability is also vital. Regular strategic planning is a good indicator of mission sustainability.

Research, research, research. When you write, adhere to the foundation's page, word, or character limitations. Be thorough but concise. Then proofread your proposal. Eliminate math, spelling, and grammatical errors that interrupt thought flow. Format numbers consistently from one section to another. Illustrate your nonprofit's mission, vision, and values consistently across the different elements of your proposal. Proofread your proposal again.

Your proposal should point to one thing: mission fulfillment. Your goal is to communicate that all organizational resources are directed at mission fulfillment. To most effectively use your time, only apply to those foundations whose missions match your nonprofit's. It is the mission impact in which the foundation is interested.

Make it easy for foundations to choose you as one of their conduits toward making progress in improving the human condition. Answer the eight questions they all have, even if they don't explicitly ask.

Other books in this series...

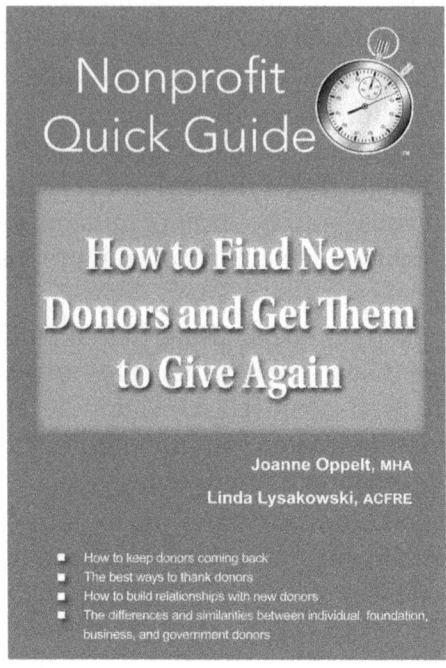

Available at leading booksellers, such as Amazon.com and Barnes & Noble.

www.ingramcontent.com/pod-product-compliance
Lightning Source LLC
Chambersburg PA
CBHW070036040426
42333CB00040B/1695